Internet Addiction

The Ultimate Guide for How to Overcome Internet Addiction for Life

presentation of the information is without contract or any type of guarantee assurance.

The trademarks that are used are without any consent, and the publication of the trademark is without permission or backing by the trademark owner. All trademarks and brands within this book are for clarifying purposes only and are the owned by the owners themselves, not affiliated with this document.

Table Of Contents

Introduction

First off, I really want to thank you for downloading this book. The pages in this book were developed through years of experiences that I have gone through, as well as what has proven to work for others that I have talked to and have researched. I also want to congratulate you for taking the time to understand your own internet addiction and how you can overcome it.

After experiencing issues with internet addiction and struggling to overcome them, I decided that I wanted to write a short, detailed ebook to help other people who are in a similar situation as I was. I also wanted to help people understand how internet addiction can be detrimental to our overall health and self-esteem. Many people have relatives or friends who struggle with internet addiction and the people around them are not able to understand what is going on in their heads.

I can guarantee that you will find this book useful if you make sure to implement what you learn in the following pages. The important thing is that you IMPLEMENT what you learn. Addictions are not conquered overnight but the important thing to remember is that it is definitely possible for you to overcome them. What I am giving you is the information you need so that you can understand your own dependent relationship with the internet, as well as the steps you will need to make that journey.

Many people experience internet addictions in their lives as it is becoming more and more necessary to be connected in today's world. A certain amount of social media use can help us to take advantage of amazing technology, but past a certain point, it becomes a leech that sucks the energy and time out of our days. As you go through these pages, you'll get a better understanding of what internet addiction really is, the signs of it, and you will learn several ways that you can overcome it. We will also dive into what work is required of you to get past the roadblocks you have.

I recommend that you take notes while you are reading this short ebook. This will ensure that you get the most out of the information in here. I want you to feel that you made a purchase that is worth your money and I want you to look over the notes of this book even after you've finished reading it. The notes will help you to pinpoint exactly what you need to implement and by writing things down, you will be able to recall specifics and how to handle certain situations when they arise.

Lastly, remember that everything in this book has been compiled through research, my own experiences, as well as the experiences of others, so feel free to question what you have read in this book. I encourage you to do your own research on the things that you want to look deeper into. The more you understand about your own mind and body, the better off you'll be. To overcome an internet addiction in your life, it will take some work on your part but you can do it! So remember to read with confidence and an open   mind!

Chapter 1:

Types of Internet Addiction

Addiction can compel an individual to spend hours on a certain activity. It is defined as a dependency on an activity, hobby or substance that can be deemed detrimental to a person's health. It can affect the individual's mental, emotional and psychological health and if the addiction continues, it can even lead to death if the addiction goes over the top without being aided.

In this book, we will discuss "Internet Addiction". This particular form of addiction happens when an individual is engrossed in using the Internet and neglects other aspects of his/her life in favor of the Internet. There are different reasons why an individual can become an Internet addict. It can be all or some of the following: One might have a cyber-sex addition, cyber-relationship addiction, computer gaming addiction, information addiction or net compulsions.

Cyber-Sex Addiction

Cyber-Sex Addiction is a form of Internet addiction wherein a person spends most of his time on pornography sites, adult chat rooms or role playing sites. Individuals who have cyber-sex addiction are believed to have frustrating relationships in life, thus making them search for other avenues to fill the gaps.

Cyber-Relationship Addiction

Cyber-Relationship Addiction happens when a person spends countless hours on social networking websites. People who are always on social media sites chatting, messaging, playing and updating their statuses are the ones who hardly have time to connect with people in real life. They spend prolonged hours in a cyber-community neglecting the real community where they belong. Reality for them has turned into a cyber-reality where all their needs are fulfilled on the Internet.

Computer Gaming Addiction

Computer Gaming Addiction explains how people are obsessed with online and offline gaming. This is quite common among teenage boys, and even a lot of adult males and females are participating in this activity. Individuals who have computer gaming addiction spend all day playing games and interacting with fellow gamers, all the while neglecting engagements and priorities.

As simple as skipping meals, staying at home and sleeping less can be aggravated if done on a regular basis. These actions happen during prolonged computer gaming hours. Computer addiction is a well-known vice among males because games are naturally engaging and filled with action. Many gaming addicts say they are even more engaging than physical activities.

Information Addiction

Information Addiction is a type of fixation where individuals spend most hours searching the web for random information. This can be about anything and everything they fancy. The Internet is a portal of endless information. It is free and easy to find any types of data online with the use of computer and basic Internet skills.

Anyone can be addicted to information because the Internet provides it with ease and liberty. People who have information addiction spend most time on their computers, typing, searching and building a community with other like-minded people. Priorities and engagements are assumed to be put aside.

Net Compulsions

Lastly, Net Compulsions focus on an individual's way of seeking money-related avenues to fulfill the gaps in their life. It can be an auction site they are obsessed with. It can be an online marketplace where one can shop using credit cards. Mostly, people who have net compulsions tend to purchase things they hardly need but bought anyway because they are on the Internet. This can cause financial-related problems and job worries.

These different kinds of Internet addictions should be understood in order to treat them specifically. The efficiency of the technology is enough of a lure to convince people to spend hours on a platform, without heeding warning to the problems it can bring.

Chapter 2:

Causes of Internet Addiction

Symptoms vary from person to person and the cure will highly depend on how much dedication one wants to put forth to recover from Internet addiction. To understand whether a person is an Internet addict or not, one should understand the person's personality. Therefore, it can be easier to distinguish the reasons of one's Internet addiction if there is a person that is close to the victim that is aware of the habits.

The first potential cause of Internet addiction is stress. A person with low tolerance to anxiety might elevate his/her stress levels without even knowing it. To be able to get through the stress, the person might seek refuge in the Internet, where gratifying information, entertainment and social community can be found. In this case, the Internet acts as a distraction, putting stress aside and dissolving it almost completely. This person will most likely go back to this pattern, knowing an easy refuge is waiting for him/her.

Depression is another cause of Internet addiction. Similar to stress, depression needs an easy and light fix to avoid aggravating the situation. The Internet provides an easy avenue for entertainment, thus making it a source of happiness, but the Internet only offers a temporary fix. The longer time a user spends online, the more he becomes acquainted to a make-believe reality that is the cyber-community. It boxes the person in to solitude and confinement. In the end, it can actually become a loss more than a gain if the person depends on the Internet for their happiness.

Lack of social support can be another reason for Internet addiction. To be able to function in the community, it is best to be acquainted with fellow individuals. The lack of social activities can truly cause sadness and the inability to express one's self in the open. Introverts tend to prefer the Internet rather than, say, a party with classmates. The cyber-community provides a society for all types of people, whether one is introverted or extroverted.

The people with less social skills find refuge online, and are more likely to spend too much time building relationships with faceless "friends" whilst neglecting the real ones around the neighborhood, because this is the easier path. This is much more dangerous for children than for adults because children and teenagers are in a stage of life where they have the ability to develop strong social skills that will change the future opportunities for the rest of their lives.

It is important to note, however, that using the Internet to meet people and develop friendships can be a powerful tool. You can connect with people who you would that you would never run into, in person. What we are discussing here is not whether developing online relationships is a good or bad thing, rather we need to realize that when a person neglects their in-person socializing for only online associations, it becomes a problem.

Unhappiness is a broad term but in the context of Internet addiction, this urges others to seek happiness online. Others prefer the companionship of cyber-community friends rather than "real" friends or acquaintances.

Others might have found like-minded people more exciting than real life friends who talk about other things. Reasons vary, but the point being is how cyber-community creates interesting cyber-people, and enough to take over the role of the physical people in everyday life.

Thus, building relationships online can be less daunting and more welcoming than doing so face-to-face in reality. This favors those who are afraid of rejection, which is why you might see people who say controversial things on the Internet that, at the same time, are too afraid to say those same exact things to a person's face.

Lastly, immobility can be a cause of Internet addiction. A person who suffered from a major accident that prevents him/her from doing any physical activities for long periods, will most likely spend hours in front of a computer, as it is so easily accessible.

It is perfectly normal to find a pre-occupation to elevate the physical and mental condition of the person. Refuge in the form of the Internet is alright; so long as the activity is monitored. The person with the disability might truly spend longer hours online due to the inability to do physical activities.

Reasons for Internet addiction vary from person to person and research is still being done on many of the core causes. The whole phenomenon of Internet addiction is still a fairly new concept because the average lifestyle for many younger people (under 35) is becoming much easier and technology seems to be more necessary each day. The combination of more free time and the focus on technology in our lives is the main factor in allowing people to become addicted.

Chapter 3:

Recognizing the Problem

As you might have guessed by now, treating Internet addiction will differ from person to person. It is better to understand what causes the addiction for an individual rather than comparing the situation to others. With Internet addiction, we want to focus on looking at the root of the problem and not focus as much on the act itself. We need to ask ourselves questions like, where is this stemming from? What hole am I trying to fill? Do I have too much free time?

The most important step to consider is to recognize the problem. When you learn the core of the problem, you will be able to trace back other dependencies that you may pick up later in life.

It does not matter whether Internet addiction affects a person psychologically, emotionally, physically or financially. The important thing is to recognize the problem and from there, the correct treatments will rightfully fall into place. If the person has the capability to understand how much the Internet is taking his/her life away, then he/she is more likely to be open to be correcting it.

Sometimes Internet addicts are too engrossed to even notice that they have a problem. This becomes another dilemma. Many times, only the people closest to the addict can attest to the addiction. These people are usually the family and friends who want a change for their loved one but do not know where to start.

If family and friends are still hesitant about discussing the problem, it is better to ask the Internet addict about it. After the discussion, it will hopefully open the person's mind towards this habit that needs to stop as soon as possible. By being polite yet thorough in the questions you ask to an Internet addict, you will get much further than you would with a confrontational approach.

Apart from recognizing the present problem, recognizing the past problems will be extremely helpful to the overall state of the person suffering from Internet addiction.

How to know if you are addicted to the Internet

You may be addicted to the Internet if you feel that personal and bugging responsibility to check any, if not all, of your social media accounts at every possible moment you can. This is the most obvious sign of addiction. From the moment you wake up, you feel the urgent need to check your account(s). You feel the need to check your mobile phone or laptop even when you are eating or when you are out with friends.

You spend most of your free time on the Internet. This is another common symptom of Internet addiction. You delay your other tasks just so you could spend your time on Facebook, Twitter, Tumblr and other social networking websites. You can spend hours on the Internet but you can't manage to keep yourself focused on some other task for even an hour. Much more than that, you lose track of time whenever you're online. Your 30-minute break becomes a two-hour one.

You are experiencing the "Did someone like my post?" syndrome. You make it a point to check your accounts to see if someone has liked or commented on your post – may it be a status message on Facebook, tweet on Twitter, or photo on Instagram.

You have this personal obligation to take a picture of almost everything and post it to your accounts; from your food, your pet dog, your new clothes, the book you're reading at the moment – you feel the need to post these photos online, especially on your social media accounts.

You share everything about anything. May it be a funny conversation among strangers that you overheard or a funny conversation between you and your friends or family, you immediately think of posting it somewhere on the Internet.

You go out of your way just to make sure you have access to your accounts anywhere you go. The most common example of this is: you look for Wi-Fi signal everywhere.

You mourn over your loss of Internet access. You feel bored whenever you're not spending your time online, and you can't manage to stay put without the Internet.

What's happening online is becoming a huge part of your life offline. When people are buzzing over a certain issue online, you feel that you must also be part of it even when you're not involved and you feel greatly affected by what's happening online.

You use Internet expressions in daily conversations. This is one of the biggest signs that you've been spending too much time on the Internet. Expressions include saying "LOL (Laugh Out Loud)" or "IDK (I don't know)" even when talking with your friends in real life. Because you use these expressions so much when you're on chat sites, you tend to include these in your daily vocabulary.

You want to get involved in almost everything regarding your social media accounts. Being unable to do so results to the uncomfortable feeling of being left out. When you haven't checked your account for two days or so, you feel that you've missed out on something big.

Do these symptoms sound familiar? Imagine that this list of symptoms is a checklist. How many have you checked? How many are you experiencing? If you have checked at least two to three things, then you're still on the normal track. However, if you are experiencing most or all of these symptoms, then it is definitely serious and something should be done.

Chapter 4:

Building Coping Skills

The Internet is a refuge. People go to the Internet not only for finding information but also for various purposes besides data gathering. They go to the Internet to make themselves feel happy by finding venues of entertainment and productivity. The Internet is the cause of much joy in the world, as well as incredible pain and bullying. The Internet has various platforms of entertainment that can be quite pleasing but can turn out to be addicting.

Examples include online gaming and online shopping. These addictions occur because online platforms continue to adjust to the demands of the consumers. Internet consumers use it because it is limitless entertainment and information rolled into one, getting better and better.

That said, the Internet becomes an alternative society where cyber-relationships are built, oftentimes pushing away real life relationships in the process. Some people prefer communities online because they pose a happier and more laid back set-up compared to real life. Families and friends of the person will most likely be put aside most of the time. On their own, they might unconsciously create a barrier that can lead to failed relationships.

Social media networks like Facebook, Twitter, Tumblr and Instagram are online platforms meant to create a community and gather like-minded people. It is an understatement to say that these sites have a big role in our world. Facebook is the most popular social networking site, garnering billions of users from around the world.

Social networking sites are more welcoming because there is less pressure to take verbal actions, which often takes more courage to do in a live interaction. People who are shy and/or scared in real life will find social networking sites a good place to test their social skills without much effort.

Embarrassment, awkwardness, and shyness will be avoided in non-face-to-face communication, or at least limited greatly. Moreover, it is a type of gratification that fulfills the need to be happy instantly, which can lead to an addictive dependency down the road.

Finding solace in social networking sites can be extremely beneficial to those who have trouble meeting people in the real world. Chatting with new found friends who have similar interests can be exciting, since people who are isolated can finally have other individuals to communicate with. However, the problem comes when individuals on social networking sites are insecure of their coping skills, and the social networks become a crutch for their own personal development.

Now, to completely overcome Internet addiction, particularly a social media addiction, a person should focus on slowly letting go of his social networking activities. Taking it one at a time will ease the panic from removing one's self from a comfortable community. This way, the person can slowly go back to his/her off-line life and focus on responsibilities, engagements and relationships that were neglected whilst being too engrossed in the Internet.

Chapter 5:

Strengthening the Support System

Internet addiction can be treated as long as the individual wants to change for the better. Acquiring a solid support system will definitely help a person deviate from too many hours on the Internet. Having family and friends around will allow real life interaction to take place, redirecting the person's attention to more realistic events. It is better to be transparent about the experiences when going through Internet addiction and allowing personal acquaintances to understand the struggles will help with accountability.

Internet addiction can be rooted from depression built from negative thought loops inside the mind. This can happen when we get into the habit of uncontrollable browsing. We begin to think too much about our own problems and searching for new content, that we lose that inner peace that we all need to think clearly. You may notice that when you've been browsing too long on the internet, you develop a hazy mind and it becomes difficult to think about the things you need to do in your own personal life.

Signing up for classes, sports teams, and pursuing social hobbies will allow the person to meet other like-minded people. Regular interaction with family, friends and new found acquaintances should be practiced as much as possible. By taking part in activities that force you to interact with others in person, you will begin to regain the balance of pursuing information and receiving feedback as well.

How to get out of an Internet addiction

Accept the fact that you are indeed addicted to the Internet. Denying that you are addicted to the Internet will only delay the recovery process. Be determined in helping yourself; do not wait for the bad effects to show up in your life before taking action.

Go out and explore the outside world. Even if you are one of those people who has already become awkward in socializing with people in real life, you must try your best to overcome it. Keep your determination intact. After all, you used to socialize with other people before you got addicted to the Internet. You just need to get back to these old habits.

Go back to your old hobbies. Do the things you used to do, like reading books, listening to music or playing sports. Once you go back to these old interests, you'll slowly find yourself losing interest in the Internet as much and you'll realize there is much more joy when you are physically involved in things. You can never fully enjoy yourself while sitting in front of a computer for hours and just looking at pictures and videos and talking to people on the Internet. Life outside the Internet is always so much better because you are receiving real life feedback.

Manage your time. Prioritize your tasks and create a strict schedule for yourself. Using social media is fine as long as it's necessary to complete your tasks, but otherwise; make it your last priority. Discipline yourself in such a way that you plan out everything that you need to do; you follow your schedule with minimum distractions and without fail.

Once you are done with all the important tasks, then you can spend some time on the Internet again. This time, you can do so without interruption or a feeling of guilt since you've already done your important tasks. Make sure to have an end time for your social media use as well. If you want to complete all your important tasks for the day by 9 o'clock and use the Internet after that, make sure to put a cap on the time you can use it or else you will stay up late and revert back to the old habits that you had.

If you really can't control your impulse to check your accounts at every possible time, it is highly suggested that you ask your best friend or the one you trust the most to change your account passwords and to keep them from you. This lessens the distraction brought about by the Internet because there is no way that you can access your accounts. This is very effective when you need to do a very important task, yet you cannot focus because you are tempted. Another strategy that is similar to this is to block the website(s) that you are addicted to and ask a person you trust to make up the password so that you can not access the sites even if you are desperate.

If you feel that social media is not doing you any good (i.e. health and personality problems), then the best thing for you to do is to delete your accounts. If all else fails, you must cut off the source of the problem before you can begin treating your Internet addiction. This way, no matter how strong and how often you feel the urge to check your online accounts, you can no longer do so because they've been deleted.

Also, once your accounts are gone, you can now focus on living your life normally and you can now try restoring your relationships with people – just like before you got addicted to the Internet. With this strategy it is important to note that you will feel a strong urge, for the first few days or even weeks, to check your favorite sites to see what new updates you have. You must ride out these urges and find something else to do in those situations. After each urge passes, you will notice that you will find it easier and easier to find joy in the real world activities again.

The tips and suggestions provided in this chapter are only useful if you put them into practice. They are very easy to say, but the actions are much more difficult. This is why the challenge for you is to follow these tips if you really want to change yourself. You cannot get out of your Internet addiction by simply staring at these plain words – there is no one who can help you, except yourself.

Remember, there is no finite time that we can use the Internet. There is always one more thing we can do on there. We can leave one more comment, look at one more picture, or watch one more video.

But when you feel yourself getting drawn in to using your accounts more than you need to, a good question to ask yourself is "In five, ten, fifteen years from now, will I be happy that I spent my time doing this or is there something I can do right now that I will be proud of?" If you can think of something your future self will be proud of, shut off the browser and get started.

Chapter 6:

Modifying the Use of the Internet

Another helpful step to overcome Internet addiction is to regulate the use of the computer. Addiction breeds from the lack of moderation, leading to excessive use of one thing. Before one knows it, the activity cannot be stopped. The habit becomes permanent and the damage has been done.

Moderating the use of the Internet may seem like a tiny step but it actually works, if done correctly. It is effective because a person will understand how prolonged hours of Internet usage are deemed useless. One will realize how these hours can be used productively, outside the confines of their cyber-community.

To moderate Internet usage, a person can start regulating strict hours for when to use the computer. Perhaps, instead of spending 6 hours straight online, one can cut it down to 3 hours. After a few days, 3 hours can be cut down to 2 hours and so on, until the person is only on the internet for completing specific tasks. The key is to apply the regulation one step at a time without repressing the person too much and forcing a binge usage.

Moreover, the person can start keeping a journal where he/she will write the time and date of the usage. The number of hours should be written down so that it can be reviewed. The journal will contain the data that can be compared from the previous days, tracking the progress of the person. The individual can do it on his/her own, provided that they will stick diligently to this process. If one is still going through difficulty of letting go of the habit completely, a family member can also help the person do the journal while guiding them through the process.

Family and close friends are more than welcome to help. They can discuss with the person about the importance of moderation and the benefits that it will bring to their life. It is also good to let the person know how supported they are in this journey. They can act as the head of the journal, jotting down observations and data while giving notes. At the end of the week, the family members or friends can talk to the person about the habits and about how improvement is taking place gradually through the diligence.

Self-Discipline

Sometimes it's difficult not to be addicted to the Internet given its wonders and the ease and convenience that it provides. Roaming around the Internet is like living in a different world, you can see different and amazing things with just a few clicks. The Internet is like a fantasy world that you can never live in, which makes it a wonderful place to be part of. However, there is no greater place than reality, as it is all we really have to come back to.

In order to balance things out, the challenge for you is to instill self-discipline in yourself. Without self-discipline, nothing can be done about your problem. Learn how to prioritize and manage your time. Eventually, you'll see for yourself that the Internet, when used wisely, is definitely one of the biggest benefits to mankind.

Conclusion

I worked hard on creating the best guide for "overcoming an internet addiction" that I could. Social media addiction was stopping me from accomplishing many things in my life. After finally overcoming my addiction, I wanted to give back to others. These are all the strategies and information that have worked for me, as well as others that I have talked to and researched. I guarantee if you stay consistent they will work for you as well. Be optimistic about your current situation and make small progress each day!

If you feel like you learned something from this book, please take the time to share your thoughts with me by sending me a message. I would really appreciate it! You can leave a a review on Amazon as well, if you'd like.

Thank you and good luck in your journey!

.